Ruby Red Dots
Fanciful Circle-Inspired Designs

By Sheri Howard

Ruby Red Dots
Fanciful Circle-Inspired Designs
By Sheri Howard

Editor: Kimber Mitchell
Designer: Bob Deck
Photography: Aaron Leimkuehler and Holly Munns
Illustration: Eric Sears
Technical Editor: Jane Miller
Production Assistance: Jo Ann Groves

Published by:
Kansas City Star Books
1729 Grand Blvd.
Kansas City, Missouri, USA 64108

First edition, first printing
ISBN: 978-1-935362-21-0

Library of Congress Control Number: 2009931384

Printed in the United States of America
By Walsworth Publishing Co., Marceline, MO

About the Author

Sheri Howard is a quilt and
doll designer who has been sewing
ever since she was old enough to hold
a needle and thread. One of her first sewing
projects was embroidering a caterpillar design that
her mother traced from a coloring book. Sheri has
designed patterns for Cotton Way for five years and her
quilt patterns have been featured in international quilt
magazines. She especially loves to appliqué and enjoys
playing with color in her designs. Sheri lives in Rexburg,
Idaho, with her husband, Cody. She sews regularly with
a circle of sewing friends that has been together for
more than 10 years. *Ruby Red Dots* is her first book.

*Sheri's necklace was made by Lori Ward
of Miss Ruby Sue.*

Table of Contents

Introduction

This book is very much a reflection of my favorite things—appliqué and the color red. And there's something about dots and circles that really speaks to me. When I was in high school, I remember hearing that no one could draw the perfect circle. During class, I would doodle in the margins of my papers trying to perfect my circle-drawing skills. Ever since then, I've been passionate about circles and dots. So it seems fitting that they often take center stage in my appliqué designs.

My love of appliqué stems from memories of my grandmother, who enjoyed making Sunbonnet appliqué quilts—the ones with the girls in big skirts hiding their faces with a parasol. She did all of her appliqué by hand with the most exquisite buttonhole stitches. As a young embroiderer at the time, I recognized the beauty in those small stitches. Although my grandmother did not teach me to sew or quilt, her quilts made a lasting impression on me. In fact, one of the first appliquéd quilts I wanted to make was a masterpiece of flowers and vines. The designers of that particular pattern used the needleturn method, but I didn't like it because I found it difficult to create perfectly round circles. Thankfully, my good friend Susan Hansen showed me a different method that makes it simpler to create near-perfect circles by using freezer paper and a fabric glue stick. Thanks to this handy technique, I was able to create crisp appliqué circles and I've been addicted to appliqué ever since. I love the freedom it gives me to create pretty projects without a lot of mathematical calculations, which is something I don't enjoy!

Most of the blocks in this book came to life in my sketchbook during travels. When I would see an object, I'd sketch it freely until I liked the design. After I fine-tuned all the shapes for the 12 blocks in the Ruby Red Dots quilt, I realized they all had one thing in common—lots of dots! And after mocking them up into a quilt design, I saw that they shared yet another theme—the color red. Imagine that! So as you can see, this book captures all the elements that speak to my heart. And I hope some part of it will speak to you as well, whether you are just starting to appliqué or you're a longtime appliquér.

Happy Sewing!

Sheri

Dedication

To my mother, Jackie Winger, who showed me how to sew at a very young age and instilled in me a lifelong passion for sewing. As a youngster, I would watch her sew and listen to her whistle in a soft whisper as she worked. I cannot recall an Easter when my sister Tracy and I did not have a new dress or a first day of school when we didn't have a new outfit. In fact, I did not have a store-bought dress until after I was married. So thank you, mom, for teaching me to sew. It has brought me more joy and satisfaction over the years than I can ever put into words.

Thanks to:

Kansas City Star Books for giving me the opportunity to write this book and showcase my work. Thanks especially to Diane McLendon for believing in my idea.

My editor, Kimber Mitchell, who has been wonderful to work with. And to the graphic designer and photographers who brought to life the images from my mind.

My quilters—Wendy Anspach, Sheri Bear, and Susan Hansen—for putting the finishing touches on the quilts. You did a beautiful job!

A special thank you to Bonnie Olaveson for asking me to design for her pattern company, Cotton Way, six years ago. This book would never have happened were it not for Bonnie, who opened up a whole new world for my creativity.

Thank you to all my sewing friends—Beth, Beverly, Chris, Kathy, Lori, Louise, LuJean, Sonja, Susan, Vikki, and Wendy. It is such a joy to sew with you every Wednesday. You have all been so supportive. I love you, ladies.

My friend Lora Zollinger, who has graciously allowed me to display my dolls and quilts in her darling shop, All Occasions, over the years.

To my sister, Tracy—one of my greatest cheerleaders. You always make me feel so smart. I am so glad we are friends. And to Cody, my husband of 30 years who has always supported my sewing pursuits and never complained. You are a quilter's dream! And last but not least, to my children—Adam, Natasha, and Holly—who are so computer-savvy. I couldn't live in this world of technology without you.

Appliqué Made Easier

With so many appliqué methods to choose from today, it's easy to find one that suits your personal tastes. For me, it's a freezer paper method that uses a glue stick to secure the fabric to the paper. To begin, cut out all the freezer paper pieces. For each piece, apply a very small amount of glue to the dull side of the freezer paper and place it on the fabric, adding a ¼" seam allowance to the fabric before cutting it out. Next, clip around the entire piece just to the paper. On the slick side of the paper, apply a ¼" line of glue to the entire edge before turning the fabric edges over on the glued portion of the slick side. This makes it easier to remove the paper from the fabric later on. To secure the appliqué pieces to the block background fabric, apply a very small amount of glue to the back of the appliqué pieces (I find this works better than trying to pin through the paper).

I machine appliqué my quilts because it is faster, but these glued pieces could easily be hand appliquéd. If you opt for my method, I recommend using an open-toe foot so you can easily see where you are sewing. This is especially important when going around corners. I like to use YLI monofilament thread because it is pliable and doesn't break easily. Needle size also makes a big difference. I use a size 60/8 needle because it makes only a very small hole in the fabric. When appliquéing, I use a very small zig-zag stitch with a 1.5 stitch length and width so the stitches are barely visible. One stitch should catch the appliqué piece and the other one should go just off it on to the background fabric (See Diagram 1 below).

When you're finished appliquéing, trim away the background fabric from the back of the block a ¼" inside the zig-zag stitch line, being careful not to cut the paper (See Diagram 2 below). Then run a large needle under the glued edges to loosen the paper. Because you used a very small stitch length, the paper is perforated, making it easier to remove. Be sure to remove the paper before layering an appliqué piece on top of another. Turn the block right side up and press, being careful not to overheat the monofilament thread. It's always a good idea to do a practice block before tackling the actual blocks that will be in your quilt. Good luck!

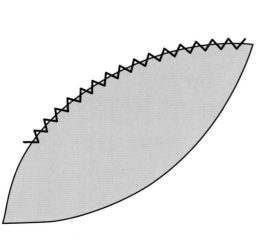

Diagram 1

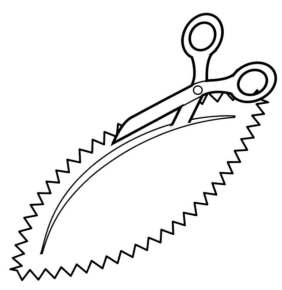

Diagram 2

Ruby Red Dots Quilt

Finished size: 87 ½" x 105 ½"
Finished block size: 12"
Machine pieced and appliquéd by Sheri Howard
Machine quilted by Wendy Anspach of The Quilt Parade

I submitted this quilt for a block-of-the-month contest sponsored by Kansas City Star Books. While brainstorming names for it, my mind focused on the "Kansas" part of their name. That in turn sparked images of Dorothy from the Wizard of Oz, who of course lived in Kansas, and her famous ruby red slippers. Combining that image with my love of dots, I suddenly thought of "Ruby Red Dots." It seemed like the perfect title for this quilt. Thanks, Dorothy, for the inspiration! Like the quilt's title, all of the blocks convey a bit of whimsy, so I took that as a cue for their names. I hope you will enjoy reading how each one got their imaginative title.

Bright Idea

Whimsy With Wool

I love working with wool because it doesn't fray and it adds a nice textural dimension to my appliqué. I often use wool circles in my designs, so that's what I chose for the dots in some of the projects featured in this book. You could easily expand the use of wool to other portions of any of these projects. For example, Valentina's baby quilt or the table runner would look enchanting made entirely of wool. For larger quilts like Ruby Red Dots, you could use wool for the appliqué shapes and cotton for the background fabrics to prevent the quilt from being too heavy. I like to mix the mediums by layering a wool piece on top of a cotton one, or vice versa. The possibilities are endless!

FABRIC REQUIREMENTS
Quantities listed are for 42" usable width, 100% cotton fabrics.

Borders and block backgrounds:
- 5 ½ yards cream print

Sashing stars:
- ¾ yard gold print with small red flowers or dots

Dots:
- 1 yard red wool or wool felt (washed and dried)

Striped sashing units:
- 1 yard green print with small red flower or dot

Striped sashing units and outer border:
- 3 yards red plaid or solid

Inner black border and binding:
- 1 ½ yard black print with small gold swirl or dot

Appliqué stems in border:
- ⅓ yard medium celery green print

Appliqué pieces:
- 5 fat quarters or scraps of red small prints, stripes, or plaids
- 1 fat quarter, plus ⅛ yard or 4" scraps of 15 different celery green to olive green small prints
- 1 fat quarter, plus ⅛ yard or scraps of 8 different mustard yellow small prints, stripes, or plaids
- 1 fat quarter, plus ⅛ yard or scraps of 5 different black small prints

CUTTING INSTRUCTIONS

All measurements include a ¼" seam allowance.

For block backgrounds in quilt center AND outer border, cut:

- 12-13 ½" squares from cream print for quilt center blocks. After they are appliquéd, trim to 12 ½" squares.
- 4-11" squares from cream print for border corner blocks. After they are appliquéd, trim to 10" squares.

For star sashing blocks, cut:

- 40-3" squares from cream print.
- 40-3" squares from gold print for star points.
- 80-2 ½" squares from cream print.
- 20-2 ½" squares from gold print for star centers.

For red-and-green striped sashing units, cut:

- 11-2 ½" strips the width of fabric from green print. Then sub-cut into 31-12 ½" strips.
- 22-2 ½" strips the width of fabric from red print. Then sub-cut into 62-12 ½" strips.

For black inner border, cut:

- 8-1 ¾" strips the width of fabric. These will be sub-cut later.

For appliqué border, cut:

- 8-10" strips the width of fabric from cream print. Sew together end to end. Then cut 2-10" x 63" strips and 2-10" x 81" strips.

For red outer border, cut:

- 9-3 ½" strips the width of fabric from red plaid. These will be sub-cut cut later.

For green stems in appliqué border, cut:

- 2-2 ½" x 27" strips from medium celery green print.
- 2-2 ½" x width of fabric strips from medium celery green print.

For appliqué pieces, cut:

- Template pieces for each block and border. Templates are on pages 48-62 (Appliqué templates are NOT reversed for fusible appliqué method. If doing needleturn appliqué, add a ¼" seam allowance to the fabric pieces).

For binding, cut:

- 10-2 ½" strips the width of fabric from black print.

ASSEMBLY DIAGRAM

BLOCK 1 Stalina

While visiting my daughter in New York City shortly after she gave birth to her daughter, I was waiting outside a local laundry mat for my clothes to finish drying when a girl wearing a white skirt with a bright yellow star design walked by. Little did she know that star would become the centerpiece for one of my quilt blocks!

Making the Block:
Cut out appliqué templates on page 48 according to cutting instructions. I like to cut my background fabric 1 inch larger than the finished block size so I can trim the block to the right size after it is appliquéd. This is because the block can pucker as it is appliquéd, resulting in a smaller size than what it started. Referring to photo above for placement, appliqué the pieces to the background fabric. Then press before trimming the block to 12 ½" square.

BLOCK 2 Leticia

Inspiration for block designs can come from the most unlikely places. This particular block is actually based on a lamp in my daughter's apartment that I noticed while visiting her. As I sketched it, the design eventually became fancier than the lamp itself!

Making the Block:
Cut out appliqué templates on page 49 according to cutting instructions. Referring to photo above for placement, appliqué the pieces to the background fabric. Then press before trimming the block to 12 ½" square.

BLOCK 3 *Jamilla Jade*

During one of my walks in the park, I noticed a woman wearing a pretty piece of jade jewelry. I began sketching it and as I continued to work on it, the design gradually became more simplified. The result of that sketch is this block.

Making the Block:
Cut out appliqué templates on page 50 according to cutting instructions. Referring to photo above for placement, appliqué the pieces to the background fabric. Then press before trimming the block to 12 ½" square.

BLOCK 4 Valentina

Valentine's Day is one of my favorite holidays. I was brainstorming quilt designs one February day when my eyes focused on a pretty Valentine's decoration. Before I knew it, that decoration became the starting point for yet another quilt block design.

Making the Block:
Cut out appliqué templates on page 51 according to cutting instructions. Referring to photo above for placement, appliqué the pieces to the background fabric. Then press before trimming the block to 12 ½" square.

BLOCK 5 Rosy Roxanna

After the birth of my granddaughter, my daughter received a beautiful bouquet of roses. Where some might see just a flower, I saw the beginnings of a charming quilt block.

Making the Block:
Cut out appliqué templates on page 52 according to cutting instructions. Referring to photo above for placement, appliqué the pieces to the background fabric. Then press before trimming the block to 12 ½" square.

BLOCK 6 *Truly Tulips*

Spring's arrival is eagerly greeted here in Idaho. When the tulips in my garden made their appearance, I sketched their cheerful silhouettes from my window and worked the pattern into my quilt.

Making the Block:
Cut out appliqué templates on page 53 according to cutting instructions. Referring to photo above for placement, appliqué the pieces to the background fabric. Then press before trimming the block to 12 ½" square.

BLOCK 7 *Delta Daneá*

While flying home from a trip to New York, I took out my sketchbook to pass the time. Looking around for some inspiration, my eyes settled on the air vent of all things. When imagination takes flight, even mundane objects like this can stimulate creative ideas. And in this case, it evoked images of a fanciful flower—the motif behind this quilt block.

Making the Block:
Cut out appliqué templates on page 54 according to cutting instructions. Referring to photo above for placement, appliqué the pieces to the background fabric. Then press before trimming the block to 12 ½" square.

BLOCK 8 Safronia

To a creative quilter's eye, a ring isn't just a pretty embellishment for the hand—
its design also looks lovely set to fabric. The marquis shape of my sapphire ring
was the muse behind this block.

Making the Block:
Cut out appliqué templates on page 55 according to cutting instructions.
Referring to photo above for placement, appliqué the pieces to the background
fabric. Then press before trimming the block to 12 ½" square.

BLOCK 9 Mirrianne

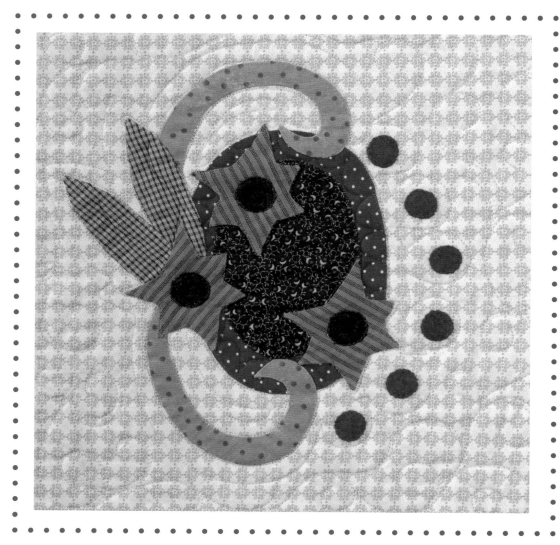

Even everyday objects can spark inspiration when you're designing a quilt. For this block, it was a pretty little oval-shaped mirror. I wanted to capture its unique shape in my quilt.

Making the Block:
Cut out appliqué templates on page 56 according to cutting instructions. Referring to photo above for placement, appliqué the pieces to the background fabric. Then press before trimming the block to 12 ½" square.

BLOCK 10 Star Sonnet

At Christmas time, our family tree sparkles with a festive assortment of ornaments. Some of these are delightful glittered stars—which gave rise to this star-studded block.

Making the Block:
Cut out appliqué templates on page 57 according to cutting instructions. Referring to photo above for placement, appliqué the pieces to the background fabric. Then press before trimming the block to 12 ½" square.

BLOCK 11 *Balia*

Believe it or not, the inspiration behind this block came from Barney, the popular purple dinosaur. While watching his show with my grandson one day, I pulled out my sketchbook. With a little imagination, Barney's head and tail evolved into this fanciful floral block. Can you see the resemblance?

Making the Block:
Cut out appliqué templates on page 58 according to cutting instructions. Referring to photo above for placement, appliqué the pieces to the background fabric. Then press before trimming the block to 12 ½" square.

BLOCK 12 *Rheema Tylina*

One day while out and about, I noticed a parked BMW. It was then I realized that their tires have the prettiest star-shaped hubcaps—yet another unexpected idea for a quilt block!

Making the Block:
Cut out appliqué templates on pages 59 and 60 according to cutting instructions. Referring to photo above for placement, appliqué the pieces to the background fabric. Then press before trimming the block to 12 ½" square.

Finishing the Quilt

SASHING

Star sashing blocks

1. Draw a diagonal line once from corner to corner on the cream print 3" squares. Repeat this step for all 40 squares.

2. Place one 3" cream print square on one 3" gold print square, right sides together. Sew ¼" from both sides of the drawn diagonal line. Repeat this step to make 40 units.

3. Cut on solid line. Make 80 half-square triangles. Press seams toward gold print. Trim half-square triangle units to 2 ½" squares.

4. Referring to the diagram below, sew 2-2 ½" cream print squares to opposite sides of one half-square triangle unit. Press seams away from center.

5. Referring to the diagram below, sew 2 half-square triangle units to the opposite sides of one 2 ½" gold square. Press seams toward center square.

6. Sew the 3 strips together to make a star block.

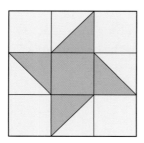

7. Press seams away from the block center. Trim units to 6 ½" square. Appliqué a red dot in the center of each star. It is important to appliqué the dot now BEFORE you combine all the pieces. Make 20 units.

Red-and-green striped sashing units

Sew a 2 ½" x 12 ½" red strip to opposite sides of one green 2 ½" x 12 ½" strip. Make 31 units. Press seams toward green print.

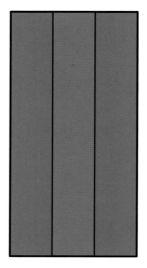

ASSEMBLING THE QUILT CENTER

1. Sew one red-and-green striped sashing unit to the left side of each of the 12 appliqué blocks.

2. Referring to the diagram below for placement, lay out all blocks and sashing units and sew units from previous step into 4 rows. Then sew one sashing strip to the end of each row. For each row, you will use 3 appliqué blocks and 4 red-and-green striped sashing units. Press seams toward the sashing.

3. Referring to the diagram below, sew one star sashing block between each of the red-and-green striped sashing units, beginning and ending with a star sashing block. For each row, you will use 4 star blocks and 3 striped sashing units. Make 5 of these strips. Press seams toward the sashing.

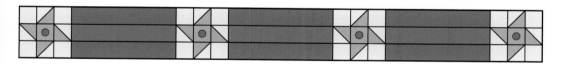

4. Referring to the diagram on the next page for placement, lay out all 9 rows. Sew rows together, beginning and ending with the star sashing strips. Press the seams of star sashing units in the opposite direction of appliquéd block seams. This completes the quilt center.

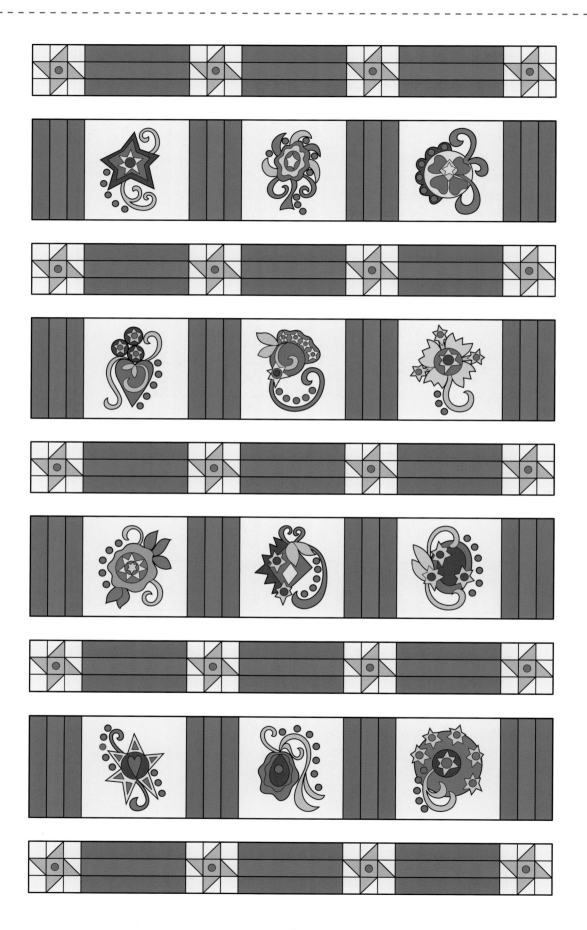

ADDING THE BORDERS

This quilt features an inner black border, a larger appliqué border and a final red border. When attaching each border, refer to the diagram on page 28 for placement.

Black inner border
1. Sew 4-1 ¾" x the width of fabric strips together end to end. Then cut 2-1 ¾" x 78 ½" strips and sew to the long sides of the quilt center. Press seams toward the black strips.

2. Sew the other 4-1 ¾" strips cut to the width of fabric together end to end. Then cut 2-1 ¾" x 63" black strips and sew to the top and bottom of the quilt center. Press seams toward the black strips.

Appliqué corner blocks
Trace and appliqué pieces on page 62 (including red wool dots) to 11" corner blocks. Press. Then trim blocks to 10" square.

Appliqué border
1. Find the center of 2-10" x 63" cream print border strips.

2. For stem in top and bottom borders, press a 2 ½" x 27" medium celery green print strip in half lengthwise.

3. Sew a scant ¼" seam allowance along the edge of strip. Find the center of the stem piece. Place the edge of the stem 4 ¾" from one side of the border, matching the centers.

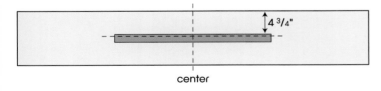

center

4. Sew on the ¼" stitched line. Turn and press stem over, covering the stitching. Appliqué both long sides of the stem with a very small zig-zag stitch. The stem should be 1" wide. Make 2 units.

5. Find the center of 2-10" x 81" cream print border strips.

6. For stem in side borders, press a 2 ½" x width of fabric medium celery green print strip in half lengthwise and repeat steps 3 and 4.

7. Referring to diagram below, appliqué all pieces (including leaves and wool dots) to the top and bottom cream print border strips. For side borders, refer to the diagram in step 9. For border templates, see page 61 (The gray templates are for the top, bottom, and side borders; white templates are for the side borders only).

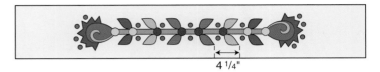

4 1/4"

8. Sew the top and bottom borders to the quilt center. Press seams toward borders.

9. Referring to the diagram below, sew two corner blocks to both ends of the long side borders. Make 2 units.

10. Sew long borders to the long sides of the quilt center, matching seams at corners. Press seams toward borders.

Red outer border
1. Sew 9-3 ½" x width of fabric strips together end to end. Press seams.

2. Measure your quilt's length and cut 2 strips to that measurement. Sew the strips to the long sides of the appliquéd borders. Press seams toward the red border.

3. Measure your quilt's width and cut 2 strips to match that measurement. Sew the strips to the top and bottom of the appliquéd borders. Press seams toward the red border.

Quilt, bind, and enjoy!

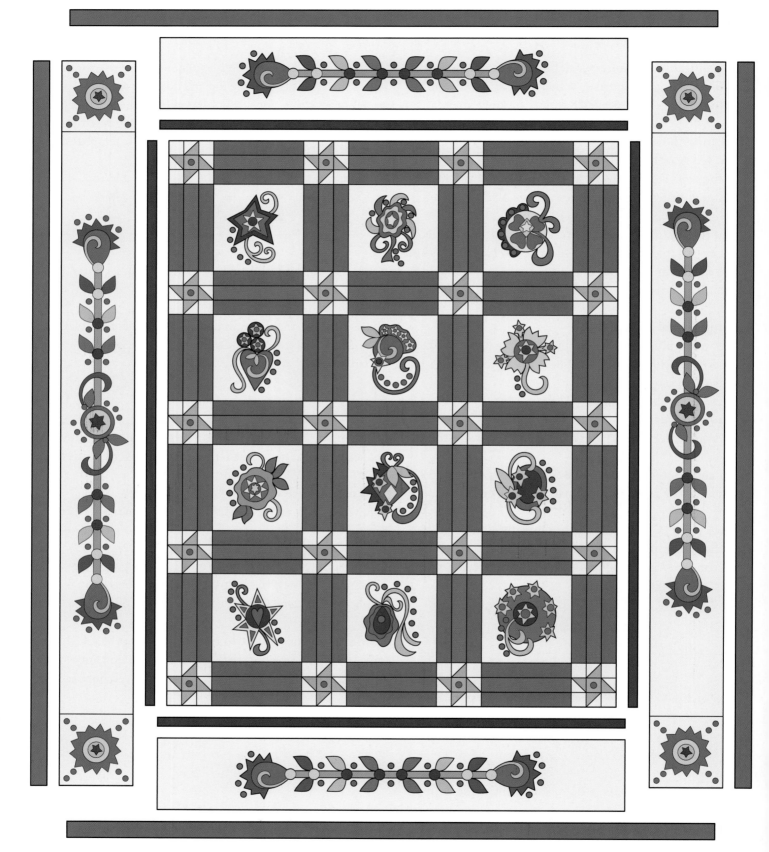

Projects

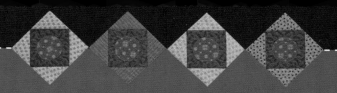

Dillia's Dots and Blocks Quilt

Finished size: *66" x 66"*
Machine pieced and appliquéd by Sheri Howard
Machine quilted by Sheri Bear of Bears Custom Quilting

Ruby Red Dots

I completed this quilt before I finished Ruby Red Dots and thought it would make the perfect companion project with its showy red circles. In keeping with the fanciful theme of the feature quilt, I gave this one a fun-loving name as well. The red and colored fabrics are from Andover Fabrics' *Jamestown* collection by Jo Morton.

FABRIC REQUIREMENTS
Quantities listed are for 42" usable width, 100% cotton fabrics.

Setting squares, triangles, large center dots, pieced border blocks, and binding:
- 2 ½ yard red-orange print

Brown blocks and borders:
- 2 ½ yard brown print with small black swirls or dots

Colored triangles, pieced border blocks, and appliqué flowers, stars, and small dots:
- ⅛ yard of 16 colored small prints such as burgundy, yellow, gold, orange, medium green, dark green, navy blue, medium blue, orange-red, tan with orange, tan with blue, tan with green, tan with navy, and green with gold

Appliqué leaves and vines:
- ⅔ yard medium green print (same as medium green listed above)

¼" bias tape maker

CUTTING INSTRUCTIONS
All measurements include a ¼" seam allowance.

For square-in-a-square blocks in quilt center, cut:
- 16-5" squares from brown print.
- 2-4 ¼" squares from each of 16 colored fabrics. Then cut each once in half diagonally from corner to corner. You should have 4 triangles of each color.

(It is important to cut these BEFORE the strips for the pieced border or you won't have enough fabric).

For red-orange setting squares in quilt center, cut:
- 2-6 ⅞" strips the width of fabric. Then sub-cut into 9-6 ⅞" squares.

For red-orange side triangles in quilt center, cut:
- 1-10 ⅜" strip the width of fabric. Then sub-cut 3-10 ⅜" squares. Next, cut each square from corner to corner twice to yield 12 triangles.

For red-orange corner triangles in quilt center, cut:
- 2-5 ½" squares. Then cut each once in half diagonally from corner to corner. You should have 4 triangles.

For flowers, stars, and dots in appliqué inner border, cut:
- 4 flower templates from blue print.
- 8 star templates from tan with orange print.
- 8 star center templates from navy print.
- 4 flower center templates from gold print.
- 4 corner dots from red print.
- 4 corner dots from gold print.
- 4 dots in border centers from red-orange print.

Templates for all these pieces are on page 63. (It is important to cut all these templates BEFORE the pieces for the pieced border blocks listed below or you won't have enough fabric. If you use a freezer paper or needleturn method, you will need to add a ¼" seam allowance to all fabric pieces).

For red circles in square-in-a-square blocks in quilt center, cut:
- 16 circle templates from red-orange print.

The circle template is on page 63. (It is important to cut these BEFORE the pieces for the pieced border blocks listed below or you won't have enough fabric. If you use a freezer paper or needleturn method, you will need to add a ¼" seam allowance to all fabric pieces).

For pieced border blocks, cut:
- 72-2 ½" squares from red-orange print for center squares in pieced border blocks

(It is important to cut these BEFORE the strips listed below or you won't have enough fabric).

- 2-1" strips the remaining width of fabric from all 16 colors. Sub-cut these strips into:
  - 10-2 ½" x 1" strips from all 16 colors.
  - 10-3 ½" x 1" strips from all 16 colors.

For appliqué inner border, cut:
- 5-8" strips the width of fabric from brown print. These will be sub-cut later.

For brown outer border, cut:
- 7-5" strips the width of fabric from brown print. These will be sub-cut later.

For green border vines, cut:
- 12-¾" bias strips for vines. Sew them together end to end to make 282" of bias. Then cut into 8-36" strips. Set aside for later. From remaining fabric, cut leaf appliqué templates on page 63.

For binding, cut:
- 7-2 ½" strips the width of fabric from red-orange print.

SEWING INSTRUCTIONS

Quilt center

1. Sew 2 colored triangles to the opposite sides of a 5" brown square. Press seams toward triangles. Make 16 units.

2. Sew 2 colored triangles to the remaining sides of the 5" brown square. Press seams toward triangles. Make 16 units. Trim blocks to 6 ⅞" square.

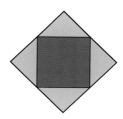

3. Appliqué a large red circle in the center of each brown square. Trim away background block fabric behind red circle to eliminate bulk. Repeat this step for all 16 blocks in the quilt center.

4. Referring to the diagram on the next page for placement, lay out all the blocks with a 6 ⅞" red square in between each block. Sew together in rows.

5. Add red setting triangles to each row.

6. Sew the 4 red triangles to the corners of the quilt center.

Ruby Red Dots

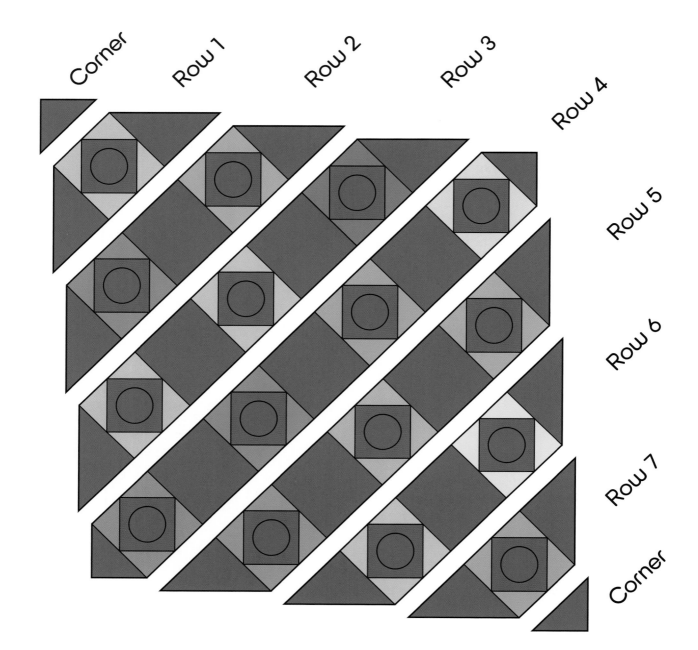

Corner Row 1 Row 2 Row 3 Row 4 Row 5 Row 6 Row 7 Corner

Brown appliqué border

1. Sew 2-8" x 36 ½" brown strips to opposite sides of the quilt center. Press seams toward borders.

2. Sew 2-8" x 51 ½" brown strips to remaining sides of the quilt center. Press seams toward borders.

Appliqué vines

1. Sew bias pieces together end to end with a bias seam.

2. Spray bias strips lightly with starch and run them through a ¼" bias tape maker.

3. Cut 4-36" strips for border corners.

4. Cut 4-32" strips for border sides.

5. Referring to the diagram, lay vines on border strip, placing the side vines over the corner vines where they intersect to hide raw ends of corner vines.

6. Appliqué vines to border strips.

7. Referring to the diagram on the next page, appliqué flowers, dots, leaves, and stars along vines.

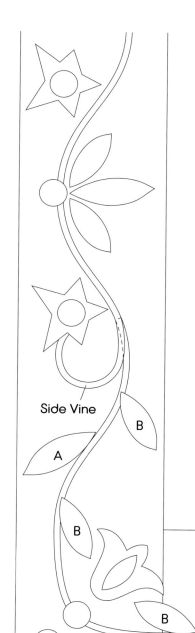

Side Vine

B

A

B

Corner Vine

B

A

B

Side Vine

A

B

A

B

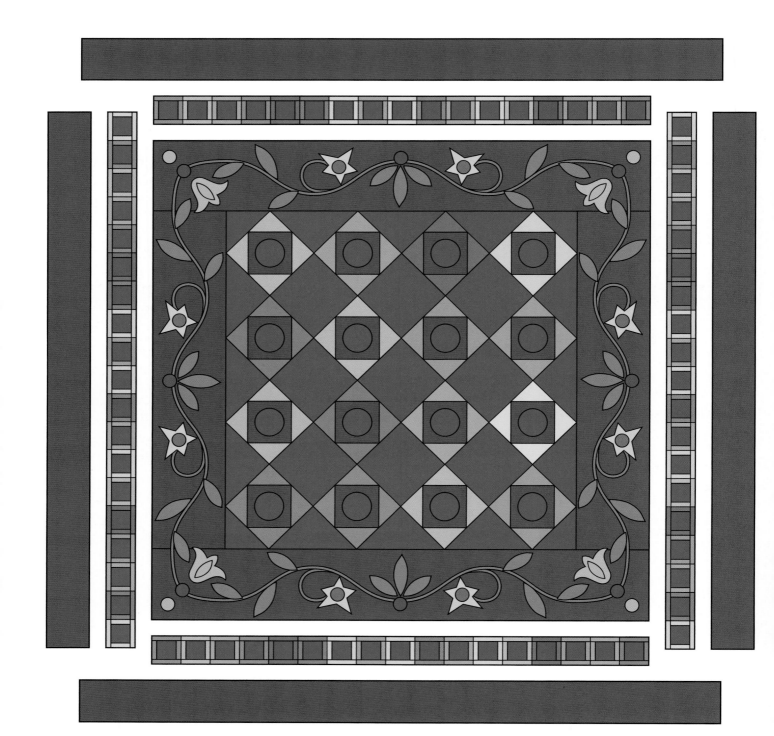

Pieced border

1. Sew 2-2 ½" x 1" colored strips to opposite sides of a 2 ½" red square. Press seams toward red block, being careful not to stretch the 1" strips. Repeat this step for all 72 blocks.

2. Sew 2-3 ½" x 1" colored strips to remaining sides of the 2 ½" red square. Press seams toward block, being careful not to stretch the 1" strips. Repeat this step for all 72 blocks.

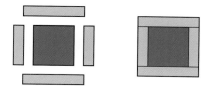

3. Sew together 17 pieced blocks in a row. Press seams in the same direction. Make 2 of these units.

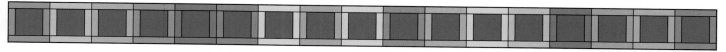

Make two with 17 blocks & two with 19 blocks

4. Sew together 19 pieced blocks in a row. Press seams in the same direction. Make 2 of these units.

5. Sew (2) 17-block strips to the top and bottom of the quilt center. Press seams toward the quilt center.

6. Sew (2) 19-block strips to the sides of the quilt center. Press seams toward the quilt center.

Brown outer border

1. Sew 7-5" x width of fabric strips together end to end.

2. Measure the width of the quilt, then cut 2 strips to that measurement. Sew to the top and bottom of the quilt center. Press seams toward borders.

3. Measure the length of the quilt, then cut 2 strips to that measurement. Sew to the sides of the quilt center. Press seams toward borders.

Quilt, bind, and enjoy!

Valentina's Baby Quilt

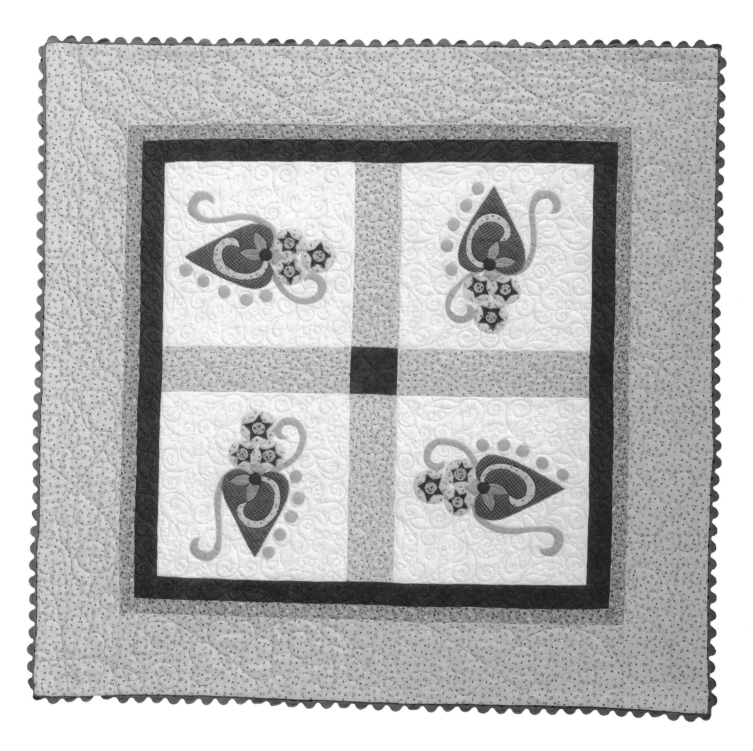

Finished size: 44" x 44"
Finished block size: 12"
Machine pieced and appliquéd by Sheri Howard
Machine quilted by Susan Hansen of Suzy Q's Quilts

If you aren't ready to tackle a large appliqué quilt like Ruby Red Dots just yet, you can easily make a scaled-down version with a single block design as shown in this quilt that spotlights four Valentina blocks from the feature quilt with a slight twist. The particular blocks used here feature an extra red dot and a diamond-like shape at the top of the heart where the two curves meet. Add a few borders, and you have a beautiful quilt without a lot of appliqué time. This charming project makes a fun gift for a special newborn as well as a cheerful wallhanging for practically any room in the home. For a fun twist, I chose pink rather than red wool for the dots in this quilt and turned the blocks in different directions.

FABRIC REQUIREMENTS

Quantities listed are for 42" usable width, 100% cotton fabrics.

Block backgrounds:
- ⅞ yard cream print

Outer border, sashing, appliqué pieces, and binding:
- 1 ¼ yards rose print with small red flowers or dots

Red border:
- ½ yard red print

Gold border:
- ¼ yard gold print with small pink flowers

Appliqué pieces:
- One fat quarter of small red check
- One fat quarter of spring green print
- Scraps of red prints
- 2" piece of rose-colored wool or wool felt for dots (washed and dried)

6 yards of red Moda© rickrack

1 yard fusible web

CUTTING INSTRUCTIONS

All measurements include a ¼" seam allowance.

For blocks, cut:
- 4-13 ½" squares from cream print. After they are appliquéd, trim to 12 ½" squares.

For sashing, cut:
- 2-3 ½" strips the width of fabric from rose print. Then sub-cut into 4-3 ½" x 12 ½" strips.
- 1-3 ½" square from red print (Cut this BEFORE red border strips listed below).

For red border, cut:
- 4-2 ½" strips the width of fabric (Cut these AFTER the red print square listed above). Then sub-cut into 2-2 ½" x 27 ½" strips and 2-2 ½" x 31 ½" strips.

For gold border, cut:
- 4-1 ½" strips the width of fabric. Then sub-cut into 2-1 ½" x 31 ½" strips and 2-1 ½" x 33 ½" strips.

For rose outer border, cut:
- 4-6" strips the width of fabric.

For appliqué pieces, cut:
- Block templates on page 64.
(To make this project go quicker, I used a fusible appliqué method. The template on page 64 has already been reversed for this method. If you use a freezer paper or needleturn method, you will need to reverse this template and add a ¼" seam allowance to all fabric pieces.)

For binding, cut:
- 5-2" strips the width of fabric.

SEWING INSTRUCTIONS

Appliqué blocks

Referring to the first diagram in the "Sashing" section for placement, appliqué pieces to cream print squares. Press well. Then trim squares to 12 ½" square.

Sashing

1. Sew a 3 ½" x 12 ½" rose print sashing strip between 2 blocks. Then sew another rose print sashing strip between the remaining 2 blocks. **Note that the appliquéd hearts are placed in different directions for each block.**

 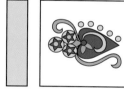

2. Sew 2-3 ½" x 12 ½" rose print sashing strips to opposite ends of a 3 ½" red print square.

3. Sew the completed sashing strip between the two rows of blocks. This completes the quilt center.

Borders

This quilt features three different borders. When attaching each border to the quilt, please refer to the diagram below for placement.

Red border

1. Sew 2-2 ½" x 27 ½" red print strips to the top and bottom of the quilt center. Press seams toward the red print.

2. Sew 2-2 ½" x 31 ½" red print strips to the sides of the quilt center. Press seams toward the red print.

Gold border

1. Sew 2-1 ½" x 31 ½" strips to the top and bottom of the quilt center. Press seams toward the gold print.

2. Sew 2-1 ½" x 33 ½" strips to the sides of the quilt center. Press seams toward the gold print.

Pink outer border

1. Sew 4-6" x width of fabric rose print strips end to end. Measure the width of the quilt. Then cut 2 strips to that measurement. Sew the strips to the top and bottom of quilt center. Press seams toward rose print.

2. Measure the length of quilt, then cut 2 strips to that measurement. Sew the strips to the sides of the quilt center. Press seams toward rose print.

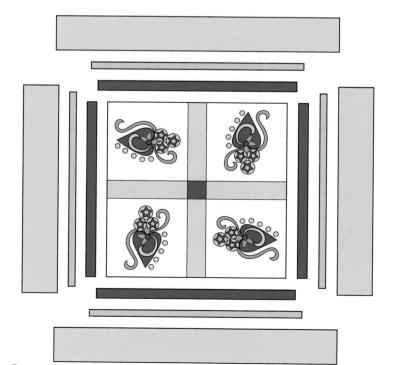

Binding and Rickrack edging

1. After the quilt has been quilted, place the rickrack so its edge is flush with the edge of the quilt. Leave a 3" tail hanging loose before starting to attach the rickrack.

2. Sew rickrack around the entire quilt, using a ⅓" seam allowance. Be careful to allow for a little extra rickrack to go around corners. End by overlapping the beginning tail with a 3" tail going off the edge to prevent loose ends.

3. Sew binding strips together end to end and press lengthwise with wrong sides together (The size of the binding strips is smaller than usual because the _entire_ binding is turned to the back of the quilt). When attaching the binding, sandwich the rickrack between the binding and quilt.

4. When finished, turn the binding _completely_ over to the back of the quilt so that the rickrack pokes out from the seam. Press binding to the back of the quilt, then whipstitch it in place.

Valentina's Baby Pillow

Finished size: 15" x 15"

This sweet pillow makes a pretty little companion for Valentina's baby quilt. Together, they are sure to brighten any nursery, but they'd also make a cozy addition to other rooms in the house. The pillow is a great gift idea for grownups, too!

FABRIC REQUIREMENTS
Quantities listed are for 42" usable width, 100% cotton fabrics.

Pillow center:
- 1-13 ½" square cream print
- 1 fat quarter muslin

Borders and pillow back:
- ½ yard rose print

Appliqué pieces:
- 5" x 6" scrap of pink print
- 3" x 14" scrap of green print
- Scraps of red print
- Scraps of gold print

One 16" x 16" pillow form

12" piece of fusible web

18" x 18" piece thin quilt batting

1 ½ yard red Moda© rickrack

CUTTING INSTRUCTIONS
For borders, cut:
- 2-2 ½" rose print strips the width fabric. Then sub-cut into 2-2 ½" x 12 ½" strips and 2-2 ½" x 16 ½" strips.

For pillow FRONT, cut:
- 1-13 ½" square from cream print.
- 1-17" square from muslin fat quarter for quilted backing of pillow front.

For pillow BACK, cut:
- 2-10" x 16" rectangles from rose print.

For appliqué pieces, cut:
- Block templates on page 64.
(To make this project go quicker, I used a fusible appliqué method. The template on page 64 has already been reversed for this method. If you use a freezer paper or needleturn method, you will need to reverse this template and add a ¼" seam allowance to all fabric pieces.)

SEWING INSTRUCTIONS
1. Referring to the photo on page 43 for placement, appliqué pieces to a 13 ½" square cream print background. Press. Then trim to 12 ½" square. Press well.

2. Sew 2-2 ½" x 12 ½" rose print strips to the top and bottom of a 12 ½" cream print square. Press seams toward rose print. Then sew 2-2 ½" x 16 ½" rose print strips to opposite sides of the 12 ½" square. Press seams toward rose print.

3. Quilt the pillow front with a thin batting, using muslin for the backing, BEFORE sewing it to the pillow back. Then trim to 16" square.

4. Sew rickrack along the entire border seam.

5. For pillow BACK, hem one 16" edge on each back piece. Lay pieces right sides up on a flat surface. Overlap the pieces on the hemmed sides until they measure 16" square. Pin together on each side.

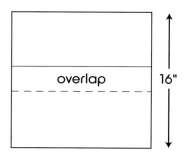

overlap   16"

6. With right sides together, place pillow back on pillow front. Pin around the edges and stitch a ½" seam around all edges. Trim corners. Turn pillow right side out and press well. Insert a 16" x 16" pillow form.

Table Runner

Finished size: 16 ¾" x 50 ¼"

Machine pieced, appliquéd, and quilted by Sheri Howard

When I was designing the Ruby Red Dots quilt, I wanted the borders to reflect its lighthearted personality without detracting from the real stars of the piece—the blocks. This simple yet enchanting design seemed to strike just the right balance. After I completed the borders, I found that they also adapted easily to a delightful table runner.

FABRIC REQUIREMENTS

Quantities listed are for 42" usable width, 100% cotton fabrics.

Background:
- ⅓ yard tan print or tea-stained muslin

Gold border:
- ¼ yard gold print with small red flowers or dots

Red border and red flowers and binding:
- ¾ yard red print with black flowers or dots

Appliqué pieces:
- 4" x 36" green stripe for stem and swirl
- 4" x 9" scraps of 3 different green prints for leaves
- 6" x 16" scraps of navy blue or black prints for flower points
- 2" piece of red wool or wool felt (washed and dried) for dots

Backing:
1 yard tan print or tea-stained muslin

CUTTING INSTRUCTIONS

All measurements include a ¼" seam allowance.

For center background, cut:
- 1-9 ¾" x 43 ¼" tan print or muslin.

For gold border, cut:
- 3-1 ¾" strips the width of fabric.

For red border, cut:
- 4-3" strips the width of fabric (Cut these AFTER the red print appliqué flowers listed below).

For appliqué, cut:
- 2 flower templates from red print (Cut these BEFORE cutting red border strip above).
- 2 flower swirls from green stripe (Cut these BEFORE cutting stem listed below).
- 1-2 ½" x 27 ½" stem from green stripe.
- 12 leaves—4 of 3 different green prints.
- 2 flower points from navy or black print.
- 4 dots from gold print.
- 2 dots from navy/black print.
- 2 dots from red print.
- 18 dots from red wool.

(The table runner uses the same appliqué templates used in the Ruby Red Dots appliquéd vining SIDE border on page 61. Appliqué templates are NOT reversed for fusible appliqué method. If doing needleturn appliqué, add a ¼" seam allowance to fabric pieces.)

For binding, cut:
- 4-2 ½" strips the width of fabric.

SEWING INSTRUCTIONS

1. To make the appliqué stem, follow Step 2 in the Ruby Red Dots appliqué border instructions on page 27. Then find the center of the tan print and the 2 ½" x 27 ½" stem piece.

2. Referring to the diagram below for placement, appliqué the pieces to the tan print or tea-stained muslin BEFORE adding the borders. Press.

3. Sew 3-1 ¾" x width of fabric gold print strips together end to end. Then sub-cut into 2-1 ¾" x 43 ¼" strips. Sew to the long sides of the table runner center. Press seams toward the gold print.

4. Sub-cut remaining gold print strip into 2-1 ¾" x 12 ¼" strips. Sew to the short ends of the table runner center. Press seams toward the gold print.

5. Sew 4-3" x width of fabric red print strips together end to end. Then sub-cut into 2-3" x 45 ¼" strips. Sew to the long sides of the table runner center. Press seams toward the red print.

6. Sub-cut remaining red print strips into 2-3" x 17 ¼" strips. Sew to the short ends of the table runner center. Press seams toward the red print.

Quilt, bind, and enjoy!

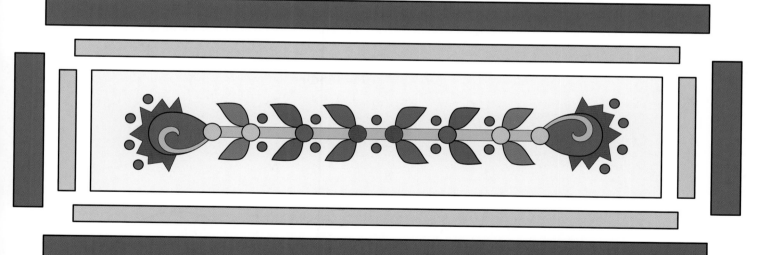

Templates

STALINA

LETICIA

JAMILLA
JADE

Join template here

Join template here

VALENTINA

ROSY
ROXANNA

TRULY
TULIPS

DELTA
DANEÁ

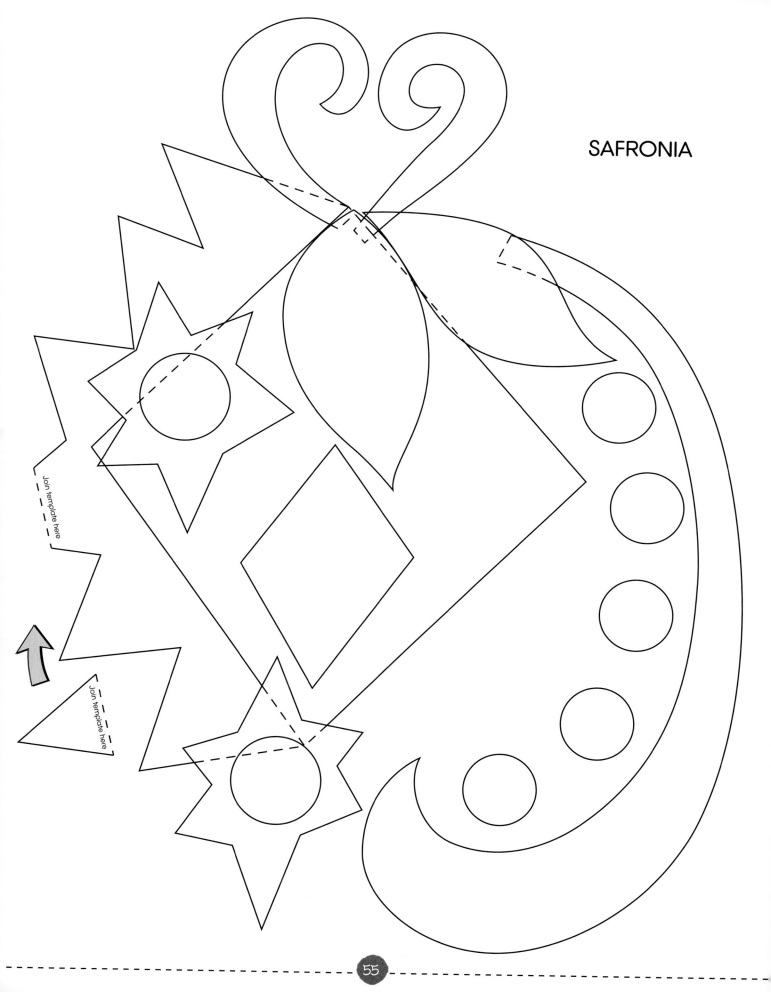

SAFRONIA

Join template here

Join template here

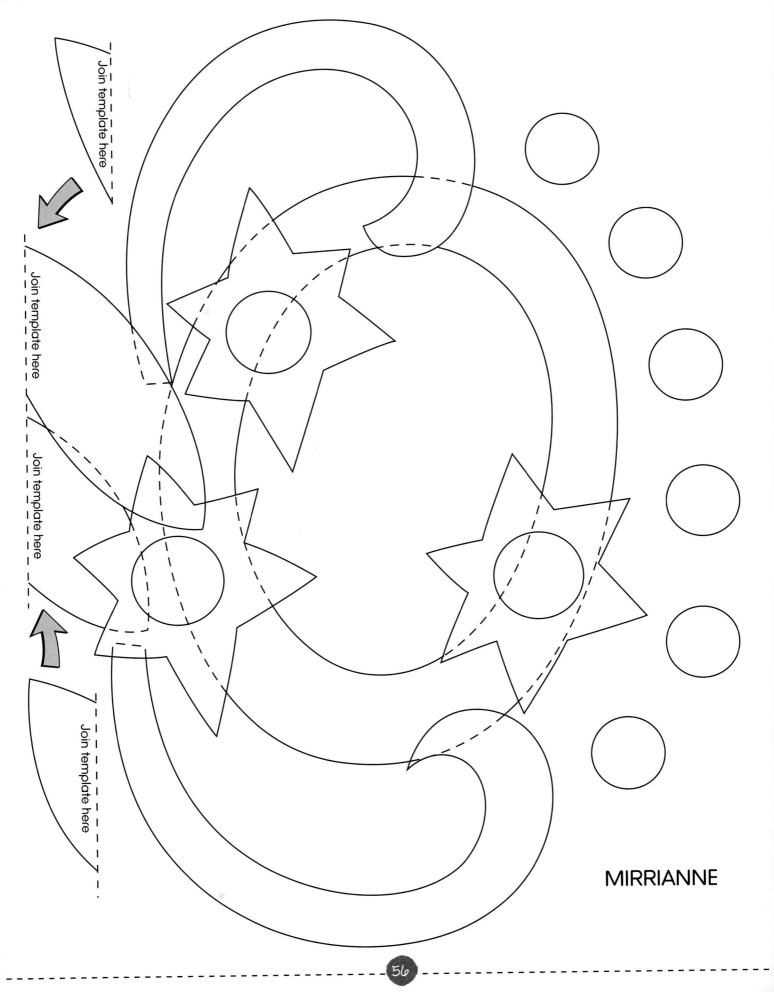

Join template here

Join template here

Join template here

Join template here

MIRRIANNE

STAR
SONNET

BALIA

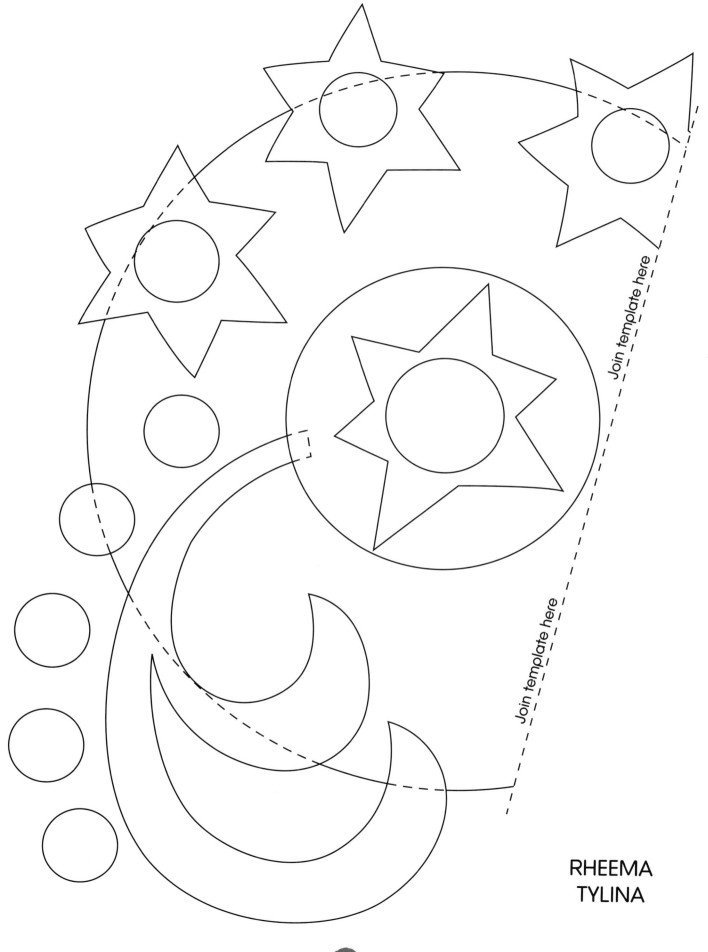

Join template here

Join template here

RHEEMA
TYLINA

RHEEMA
TYLINA

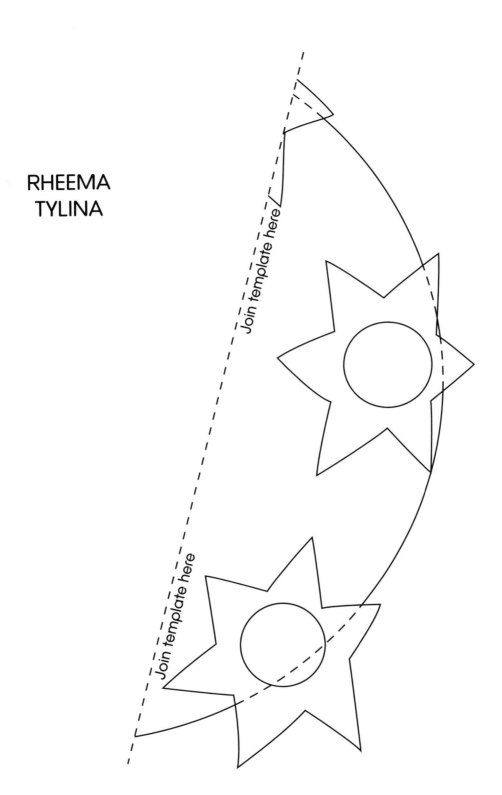

Join template here

Join template here

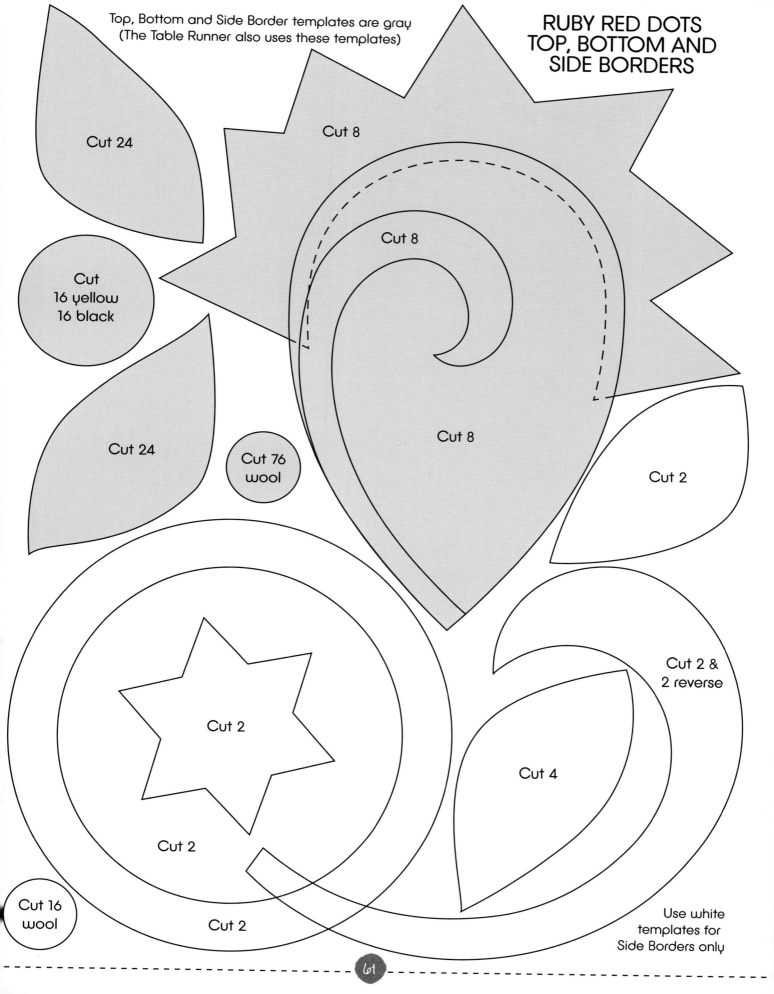

Top, Bottom and Side Border templates are gray
(The Table Runner also uses these templates)

RUBY RED DOTS
TOP, BOTTOM AND
SIDE BORDERS

Cut 24

Cut 8

Cut 8

Cut 8

Cut
16 yellow
16 black

Cut 24

Cut 76
wool

Cut 2

Cut 2 &
2 reverse

Cut 2

Cut 2

Cut 4

Cut 16
wool

Cut 2

Use white
templates for
Side Borders only

RUBY RED DOTS
CORNER BORDER
BLOCKS

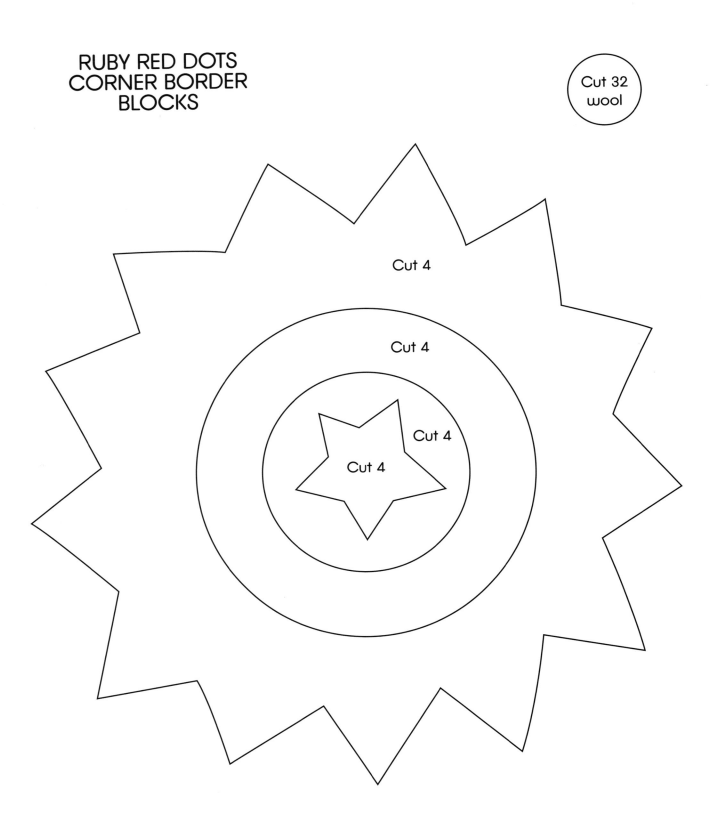

Cut 32
wool

Cut 4

Cut 4

Cut 4

Cut 4

Cut 4

DILLIA'S DOTS AND BLOCKS BORDER

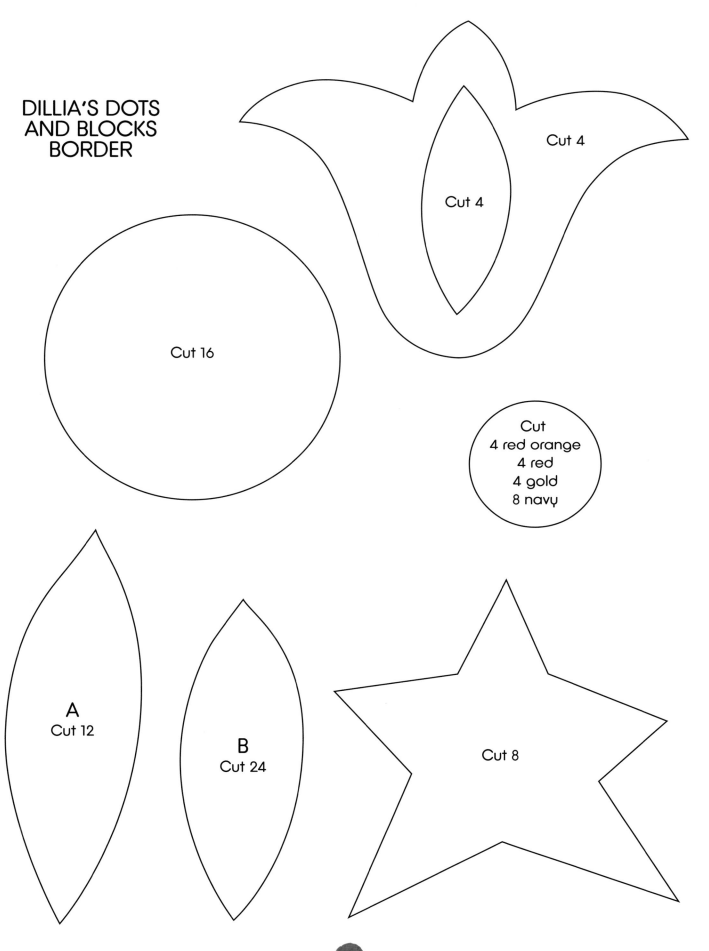

Cut 4

Cut 4

Cut 4

Cut 16

Cut
4 red orange
4 red
4 gold
8 navy

A
Cut 12

B
Cut 24

Cut 8

VALENTINA'S
BABY QUILT
AND PILLOW